DIABETIC

AIR FRYER

COOKBOOK
FOR BEGINNERS

How to Enhance Your Diet with Quick, Heart-Healthy
Recipes for a Balanced Meal Plan Under 1500 Calories a Day

Includes Diabetic Food Chart
And
Bonus 7 Day Meal Plan
Customized For Your Needs

By Bella Flowers

This Cookbook is For:

- **Prediabetics and Diabetics (Type I and II)**: Whether you are newly diagnosed or have been managing diabetes for years, these recipes are tailored to help you maintain a balanced diet and keep your blood sugar levels stable.

- **Women Above 50**: Recognizing the unique dietary needs and health concerns of women in this age group, our 7-Day Meal Plan is specifically designed for women aiming to stay under 1500 calories per day. Additionally, we offer bonus access to personalized meal plans tailored to your needs, complete with an automated grocery shopping list. These plans support heart health, bone density, and overall well-being.

- **Anyone Interested in Healthy Food**: Even if you are not diabetic, but are looking for nutritious, delicious recipes, cooked with your air fryer, this cookbook provides heart-healthy options that anyone can enjoy.

Our goal is to make healthy eating accessible, enjoyable, and beneficial for everyone, helping you to lead a healthier life through thoughtful, well-balanced meals.

DISCLAMER

The information provided in this book is for educational purposes only and is not intended as medical advice. Always consult with a healthcare professional before making any significant changes to your diet or eating routine.

ISBN: 9798334308459

Contents

Understanding Diabetes

Diabetes is a chronic condition that affects how your body processes blood sugar (glucose). Proper management of diabetes involves careful attention to your diet to maintain stable blood sugar levels. Here's a closer look at how different macronutrients—carbohydrates, proteins, and fats—affect your blood sugar and insulin levels:

Carbohydrates

Carbohydrates have the most significant impact on blood sugar levels. When you eat carbohydrates, your body breaks them down into glucose, which enters the bloodstream. This triggers the release of insulin, a hormone that helps cells absorb glucose for energy. For diabetics, it's crucial to manage carbohydrate intake to avoid spikes in blood sugar. Our recipes emphasize low-carb options to help maintain steady glucose levels.

Proteins

Proteins are essential for building and repairing tissues, and they have a relatively minor effect on blood sugar. However, they can influence insulin levels indirectly. Consuming protein along with carbohydrates can slow the absorption of sugar, leading to more stable blood glucose levels. This cookbook includes balanced recipes with adequate protein to support muscle health and overall nutrition.

Fats

Fats have the least immediate impact on blood sugar but play a vital role in overall health. Healthy fats, such as those from avocados, nuts, and olive oil, can improve insulin sensitivity and reduce inflammation. Including healthy fats in your diet can help you feel satisfied and manage your weight, which is important for diabetes control. Our recipes incorporate good fats to support heart health and satiety.

Managing Blood Sugar and Insulin

Maintaining stable blood sugar levels involves balancing your intake of these macronutrients throughout the day. By choosing foods with a low glycemic index (GI), you can prevent rapid spikes in blood sugar. The recipes in this cookbook are designed to have a low to moderate GI, making them suitable for managing diabetes.

The Importance of Water

Proper hydration is crucial for everyone, especially those managing diabetes. Water helps regulate blood sugar levels by aiding in the removal of excess glucose through urine. It also supports overall metabolic functions and prevents dehydration, which can affect blood sugar control. This cookbook includes an hourly, daily, and weekly water consumption guide reflected in our 1 week meal plan, ensuring you stay well-hydrated alongside your meals.

By understanding how different foods affect your body, you can make better dietary choices to manage diabetes effectively. The recipes in this cookbook are meticulously selected to meet the nutritional needs of diabetics, providing a variety of tasty options that support stable blood sugar and overall health.

Mastering Diabetes with Air Frying Cooking

Why Air Fryers Are Your Best Friend

Air fryers have revolutionized the way we approach healthy eating, especially for those managing diabetes. These versatile kitchen appliances use hot air circulation to cook food, allowing you to achieve a crispy texture with significantly less oil compared to traditional frying methods. This makes it easier to enjoy your favorite fried foods without compromising your health.

Benefits of Heart-Healthy Recipes

Heart health is particularly important for diabetics, who are at a higher risk for cardiovascular disease. Heart-healthy recipes typically emphasize:

- Reduced Saturated and Trans Fats: Helps maintain healthy cholesterol levels.
- Low Sodium: Helps control blood pressure.
- Rich in Omega-3 Fatty Acids: Beneficial for heart health, found in fish, flaxseeds, and walnuts.

Tips and Tricks for Best Results with Your Air Fryer

- Preheating: Preheat the air fryer for 3-5 minutes for optimal cooking.
- Do Not Overcrowd: Arrange food in a single layer for even air circulation.
- Shake or Flip Food: Shake the basket or flip food halfway through for even browning.
- Oil Sprays: Use oil spray for a light coating to enhance crispiness without adding excess calories.
- Use Parchment Paper: Place perforated parchment paper in the basket to prevent sticking and ease cleanup.

Cleaning and Maintenance

- Regular Cleaning: Clean the basket and pan after each use with warm soapy water.
- Remove Residue: Use a soft brush or cloth to remove food residue from the heating element.
- Avoid Abrasives: Do not use metal utensils or abrasive cleaners, as they can damage the non-stick coating.
- Periodic Deep Cleaning: Occasionally remove all parts and wash them thoroughly for a deep clean.

By incorporating an air fryer into your cooking routine, you can enjoy a variety of delicious, diabetes-friendly meals that support your overall health and well-being.

Why Choose This Cookbook

Managing diabetes doesn't have to mean sacrificing flavor or convenience. This cookbook is designed to help you improve your diet. Whether you're new to diabetes management or looking to simplify your meal preparation, you'll find delicious recipes that fit seamlessly into your lifestyle. Here are the reasons why this cookbook is your perfect choice:

- Simple and Practical: Our delicious, heart-healthy recipes are created for a small air fryer, making them quick and easy to prepare. The two-serving format ensures you cook just what you need, reducing waste and keeping portions in check.

- Colorful Illustrations: Each recipe is illustrated with a full-color image to give you an idea of the final result.

- Targeted Nutrition: Each recipe includes detailed nutritional information, including calories, carbohydrates, fats, and proteins. This allows you to make informed choices that align with your dietary goals.

- Printable Diabetic Food Chart: The bonus printable food chart provides a handy reference for your nutritional needs. You can find it at the back of your cookbook or request a link for a printable download.

- Comprehensive Meal Plans: The included 7-day sample meal plan, tailored to stay under 1500 calories per day, helps you maintain a balanced diet. Plus, a grocery shopping list is included.

- Customization: Along with the meal plans, you receive a customizable Google spreadsheet to create personalized meal plans. You can control your ingredient list, recipes, and create an automatic meal plan with an automatic shopping list.

- Support: Join our Facebook group to find the newest recipes, connect with other readers, share experiences, and get additional support.

Navigate with Ease

Our cookbook is user-friendly, with indexed recipes and ingredients that make it easy to find specific dishes or components. A comprehensive food chart at the back of the cover and an electronic PDF version provide quick references for nutritional information, ensuring you have everything you need to make informed dietary choices every day.

BREAKFAST RECIPES

Banana Oat Muffins

Yield: 2 servings | **Prep time:** 10 minutes | **Cook time:** 15 minutes

Ingredients:
1 ripe banana, mashed
1/2 cup oats
1/4 cup Greek yogurt
1 egg
1/2 tsp baking powder
1/4 tsp cinnamon
1 tbsp honey (optional)

Directions:
Preheat the air fryer to 320°F (160°C).
In a bowl, mix all ingredients until well combined.
Spoon the batter into silicone muffin cups.
Place the muffin cups in the air fryer basket and cook for 12-15 minutes, or until a toothpick comes out clean.
Cool before serving.

Nutritional Info: approximately 150 calories, 25g carbs, 4g fats

Zucchini Fritters

Yield: 2 servings | **Prep time:** 10 minutes | **Cook time:** 10 minutes

Ingredients:
2 medium zucchinis, grated and excess water squeezed out
1 egg
1/4 cup whole wheat flour
1/4 cup grated Parmesan cheese
1 clove garlic
Salt and pepper to taste
Cooking spray

Directions:
Preheat the air fryer to 375°F (190°C).
In a bowl, mix the grated zucchini, egg, flour, Parmesan cheese, crushed garlic, salt, and pepper.
Form the mixture into small patties and place them in the air fryer basket.
Lightly spray with cooking spray and cook for 8-10 minutes, flipping halfway through, until golden brown.
Serve warm.

Nutritional Info: approximately 170 calories, 18g carbs, 12g protein, 6g fats

Veggie Frittata

| Yield: 2 servings | Prep time: 10 minutes | Cook time: 15 minutes |

Ingredients:
4 large eggs
1/2 cup diced bell peppers
1/2 cup diced tomatoes
1/4 cup diced onions
1/4 cup shredded low-fat cheese
Salt and pepper to taste
Cooking spray

Directions:
Preheat the air fryer to 320°F (160°C).
In a bowl, whisk the eggs and mix in the bell peppers, tomatoes, onions, cheese, salt, and pepper.
Spray a small, oven-safe dish with cooking spray and pour in the egg mixture.
Place the dish in the air fryer and cook for 12-15 minutes, or until the eggs are set.
Serve warm.

Nutritional Info: approximately 200 calories, 7g carbs, 17g protein, 12g fats

Fluffy Scrambled Eggs with Spinach and Feta

| Yield: 2 servings | Prep time: 10 minutes | Cook time: 10 minutes |

Ingredients:
4 large eggs
1 cup fresh spinach, chopped
1/4 cup feta cheese, crumbled
Salt and pepper to taste
Cooking spray

Directions:
Preheat your air fryer to 300°F (150°C).
In a bowl, whisk the eggs until well beaten. Stir in the chopped spinach and crumbled feta cheese. Season with salt and pepper to taste.
Spray a small, oven-safe dish with cooking spray. Pour the egg mixture into the dish.
Place the dish in the air fryer and cook for 8-10 minutes, or until the eggs are set and fully cooked.
Serve warm.

Nutritional Info: approximately 194 calories, 2g carbs, 16g protein, 14g fats

Breakfast Burritos

Yield: 2 servings | **Prep time:** 10 minutes | **Cook time:** 10 minutes

Ingredients:
2 whole-grain tortillas
4 large eggs
1/2 cup black beans, rinsed and drained
1/4 cup salsa
1/4 cup shredded low-fat cheese
Cooking spray

Directions:
Preheat the air fryer to 350°F (175°C).
In a non-stick skillet, scramble the eggs until fully cooked.
Divide the eggs, black beans, salsa, and cheese between the tortillas.
Roll up the tortillas and place them in the air fryer basket seam-side down. Lightly spray with cooking spray.
Cook for 5-7 minutes, until the tortillas are crispy.
Serve warm.

Nutritional Info: approximately 300 calories, 30g carbs, 12g fats

Blueberry Pancakes

Yield: 2 servings | **Prep time:** 10 minutes | **Cook time:** 10 minutes

Ingredients:
1 cup whole wheat pancake mix
1/2 cup water
1/2 cup fresh blueberries
Cooking spray

Directions:
Preheat the air fryer to 320°F (160°C).
In a bowl, mix the pancake mix and water until smooth, then fold in the blueberries.
Spray a small, oven-safe dish with cooking spray and pour in the batter.
Place the dish in the air fryer and cook for 8-10 minutes, or until the pancakes are cooked through.
Let cool before serving.

Nutritional Info: approximately 180 calories, 30g carbs, 4g fats

Avocado Egg Cups

Yield: 2 servings	Prep time: 5 minutes	Cook time: 12 minutes

Ingredients:	Directions:
1 ripe avocado, halved and pitted 2 large eggs Salt and pepper to taste Cooking spray	Preheat the air fryer to 350°F (175°C). Scoop out a bit of the avocado flesh to create a larger well for the eggs. Crack an egg into each avocado half and season with salt and pepper. Lightly spray the air fryer basket with cooking spray and place the avocado halves inside. Cook for 10-12 minutes, or until the eggs are cooked to your desired doneness. Serve warm.

Nutritional Info: approximately 250 calories, 12g carbs, 20g fats

Cauliflower Hash Browns

Yield: 2 servings	Prep time: 10 minutes	Cook time: 15 minutes

Ingredients:	Directions:
2 cups riced cauliflower 1/4 cup grated Parmesan cheese 1 egg 1/4 tsp garlic powder 1/4 tsp onion powder Salt and pepper to taste Cooking spray	Preheat the air fryer to 375°F (190°C). In a bowl, mix the riced cauliflower, Parmesan cheese, egg, garlic powder, onion powder, salt, and pepper. Form the mixture into small patties and place them in the air fryer basket. Lightly spray with cooking spray and cook for 12-15 minutes, flipping halfway through, until golden brown. Serve warm.

Nutritional Info: Approximately 100 calories, 5g carbs, 9g protein, 5g fats

Egg White Bites

Yield: 2 servings	Prep time: 5 minutes	Cook time: 10 minutes

Ingredients:
1 cup egg whites
1/4 cup diced bell peppers
1/4 cup diced tomatoes
1/4 cup shredded low-fat cheese
Salt and pepper to taste
Cooking spray

Directions:
Preheat the air fryer to 320°F (160°C).
In a bowl, mix the egg whites, bell peppers, tomatoes, cheese, salt, and pepper.
Spray silicone muffin cups with cooking spray and pour the egg mixture into the cups.
Place the muffin cups in the air fryer basket and cook for 10-12 minutes, or until the egg whites are set.
Let cool before serving.

Nutritional Info: approximately 80 calories, 3 carbs, 10g protein, 3g fats

Almond Flour Waffles

Yield: 2 servings	Prep time: 10 minutes	Cook time: 10 minutes

Ingredients:
1 cup almond flour
2 large eggs
1/4 cup unsweetened almond milk
1 tbsp melted coconut oil
1 tsp baking powder
1/2 tsp vanilla extract
Cooking spray

Directions:
Preheat the air fryer to 320°F (160°C).
In a bowl, mix all ingredients until well combined.
Spray a small, oven-safe dish with cooking spray and pour in the batter.
Place the dish in the air fryer and cook for 8-10 minutes, or until the waffles are cooked through.
Let cool before serving.

Nutritional Info: Approximately 200 calories, 6g carbs, 8g protein, 16g fats

Cheesy Broccoli Omelette

Yield: 2 servings | **Prep time:** 10 minutes | **Cook time:** 10 minutes

Ingredients:
4 large eggs
1/2 cup steamed broccoli, chopped
1/4 cup shredded low-fat cheese
Salt and pepper to taste
Cooking spray

Directions:
Preheat the air fryer to 320°F (160°C).
In a bowl, whisk the eggs and mix in the broccoli, cheese, salt, and pepper.
Spray a small, oven-safe dish with cooking spray and pour in the egg mixture.
Place the dish in the air fryer and cook for 8-10 minutes, or until the eggs are set.
Serve warm.

Nutritional Info: Approximately 180 calories, 5g carbs, 13g protein, 12g fats

Coconut Flour Pancakes

Yield: 2 servings | **Prep time:** 10 minutes | **Cook time:** 10 minutes

Ingredients:
1/4 cup coconut flour
2 large eggs
1/4 cup unsweetened almond milk
1 tbsp melted coconut oil
1/2 tsp baking powder
1/2 tsp vanilla extract
Cooking spray

Directions:
Preheat the air fryer to 320°F (160°C).
In a bowl, mix all ingredients until well combined.
Spray a small, oven-safe dish with cooking spray and pour in the batter.
Place the dish in the air fryer and cook for 8-10 minutes, or until the pancakes are cooked through.
Let cool before serving.

Nutritional Info: Approximately 180 calories, 85g carbs, 14g protein, 12g fats

Whole Wheat Avocado Toast with Eggs

Yield: 2 servings | **Prep time:** 10 minutes | **Cook time:** 10 minutes

Ingredients:
2 slices whole wheat bread
1 avocado, mashed
2 large eggs
Salt and pepper to taste
Cooking spray

Directions:
Preheat the air fryer to 360°F (180°C).
Lightly spray the bread with cooking spray and place in the air fryer. Toast for 3-4 minutes.
While the bread is toasting, poach the eggs.
Spread mashed avocado on the toasted bread, top with poached eggs, and season with salt and pepper.

Nutritional Info: Approximately 280 calories, 25g carbs, 15g protein, 18g fats

Kale and Avocado Breakfast Chips with Berries

Yield: 2 servings | **Prep time:** 10 minutes | **Cook time:** 10 minutes

Ingredients:
1 cup fresh kale, chopped
1 avocado, sliced
1 cup mixed berries
1 tbsp olive oil
Salt and pepper to taste

Directions:
Preheat the air fryer to 350°F (175°C).
Toss the kale with olive oil, salt, and pepper.
Place the kale in the air fryer basket and cook for 5-7 minutes, or until crispy.
Serve the kale chips with sliced avocado and mixed berries.

Nutritional Info: Approximately 180 calories, 15g carbs, 3g proteins, 14g fats

Stuffed Bell Peppers with Eggs

Yield: 2 servings | **Prep time:** 10 minutes | **Cook time:** 15 minutes

Ingredients:
2 bell peppers, halved and seeds removed
4 large eggs
1/4 cup diced tomatoes
1/4 cup shredded low-fat cheese
Salt and pepper to taste
Cooking spray

Directions:
Preheat the air fryer to 350°F (175°C).
Place the bell pepper halves in the air fryer basket and cook for 5 minutes to soften.
Crack an egg into each bell pepper half and top with diced tomatoes, cheese, salt, and pepper.
Cook for an additional 10 minutes, or until the eggs are cooked to your desired doneness.
Serve warm.

Nutritional Info: Approximately, 150 calories, 7g carbs, 12g protein, 8g fats

Quinoa Breakfast Bowl with Spinach and Tofu

Yield: 2 servings | **Prep time:** 15 minutes | **Cook time:** 15 minutes

Ingredients:
1 cup cooked quinoa
1/2 cup fresh spinach, chopped
1/2 cup firm tofu, cubed
1 tbsp olive oil
Salt and pepper to taste

Directions:
Preheat the air fryer to 350°F (175°C).
Toss the tofu with olive oil, salt, and pepper.
Place the tofu in the air fryer basket and cook for 10-12 minutes, or until golden.
In a bowl, combine cooked quinoa, spinach, and air-fried tofu.
Season with additional salt and pepper if needed.

Nutritional Info: Approximately 280 calories, 28g carbs, 12g proteins, 14g fats

Cauliflower Rice with Sautéed Kale and Eggs

Yield: 2 servings | **Prep time:** 10 minutes | **Cook time:** 15 minutes

Ingredients:
2 cups cauliflower rice
1 cup fresh kale, chopped
2 large eggs
1 tbsp olive oil
Salt and pepper to taste
Cooking spray

Directions:
Preheat the air fryer to 350°F (175°C).
Toss the cauliflower rice and kale with olive oil, salt, and pepper.
Place the mixture in an oven-safe dish and cook in the air fryer for 10-12 minutes.
Meanwhile, fry the eggs in a pan with cooking spray.
Serve the cauliflower rice and kale topped with fried eggs.

Nutritional Info: Approximately 220 calories, 10g carbs, 10g proteins, 16g fats

Turkey and Spinach Wrap with Tortilla

Yield: 2 servings | **Prep time:** 10 minutes | **Cook time:** 10 minutes

Ingredients:
2 whole wheat tortillas
4 slices turkey breast
1/2 cup fresh spinach, chopped
1/4 cup shredded low-fat cheese
Cooking spray

Directions:
Preheat the air fryer to 360°F (180°C).
Place turkey, spinach, and cheese on each tortilla and roll up tightly.
Lightly spray the wraps with cooking spray and place in the air fryer basket.
Cook for 5-7 minutes, or until the tortillas are crispy and the cheese is melted.

Nutritional Info: Approximately 250 calories, 28g carbs, 20g protein, 10g fats

Barley and Berry Breakfast Salad with Nuts

Yield: 2 servings | **Prep time:** 10 minutes | **Cook time:** 10 minutes

Ingredients:
1 cup cooked barley
1 cup mixed berries
1/4 cup chopped nuts (e.g., almonds, walnuts)
1 tbsp olive oil
1 tbsp lemon juice
Salt and pepper to taste

Directions:
Preheat the air fryer to 350°F (175°C).
Toss the cooked barley with olive oil, lemon juice, salt, and pepper.
Place the barley in an oven-safe dish and cook in the air fryer for 8-10 minutes.
In a bowl, combine the air-fried barley, mixed berries, and nuts.

Nutritional Info: Approximately 300 calories, 40g carbs, 8g protein, 14g Fats

Oats and Apple Porridge with Cinnamon

Yield: 2 servings | **Prep time:** 5 minutes | **Cook time:** 20 minutes

Ingredients:
1 cup rolled oats
1 apple, diced
2 cups water
1 tsp cinnamon
1 tbsp honey (optional)

Directions:
Preheat the air fryer to 300°F (150°C).
In an oven-safe dish, combine oats, apple, water, and cinnamon.
Place the dish in the air fryer and cook for 18-20 minutes, stirring occasionally.
Drizzle with honey before serving, if desired.

Nutritional Info: Approximately 210 calories, 40g carbs, 5g proteins, 3g fats

Egg and Spinach Muffins with Low-Fat Yogurt

Yield: 2 servings | **Prep time:** 10 minutes | **Cook time:** 15 minutes

Ingredients:
3 large eggs
1/4 cup fresh spinach, chopped
1/4 cup low-fat cheese, shredded
Salt and pepper to taste
Cooking spray
1 cup low-fat yogurt

Directions:
Preheat the air fryer to 320°F (160°C).
In a bowl, whisk the eggs and mix in the spinach, cheese, salt, and pepper.
Spray muffin tins with cooking spray and pour the egg mixture into each cup.
Place the muffin tins in the air fryer and cook for 12-15 minutes, or until the eggs are set.
Serve warm with a side of low-fat yogurt.

Nutritional Info: Approximately 150 calories, 3g carbs, 12g proteins, 10g fats

Tofu Scramble with Broccoli and Kale

Yield: 2 servings | **Prep time:** 10 minutes | **Cook time:** 15 minutes

Ingredients:
1 cup firm tofu, crumbled
1/2 cup steamed broccoli, chopped
1/2 cup fresh kale, chopped
1 tbsp olive oil
1/2 tsp turmeric
Salt and pepper to taste
Cooking spray

Directions:
Preheat the air fryer to 350°F (175°C).
Toss the crumbled tofu with olive oil, turmeric, salt, and pepper.
Place the tofu in the air fryer basket and cook for 10-12 minutes, shaking halfway through.
In the last 3 minutes of cooking, add the broccoli and kale to the air fryer basket.
Serve warm.

Nutritional Info: Approximately 180 calories, 8g carbs, 14g proteins, 12g fats

LUNCH RECIPES

Turkey Sausage Patties

Yield: 2 servings | **Prep time:** 10 minutes | **Cook time:** 10 minutes

Ingredients:
1/2 lb ground turkey
1 clove garlic
1/2 diced onion
1/2 tsp dried sage
Black pepper and salt to taste

Directions:
Preheat the air fryer to 375°F (190°C).
Crash garlic and mix all ingredients in a bowl. Form into 4 patties.
Place patties in the air fryer basket and cook for 8-10 minutes, flipping halfway through.
Serve warm.

Nutritional Info: Approximately 200 calories, 3g carbs, 10g fats, 26g protein

Stuffed Bell Peppers with Quinoa and Spinach

Yield: 2 servings | **Prep time:** 15 minutes | **Cook time:** 15 minutes

Ingredients:
2 bell peppers, tops cut off and seeds removed
1/2 cup cooked quinoa
1/2 cup fresh spinach, chopped
1/4 cup crumbled feta cheese
2 tbsp diced red onion
1 clove garlic, minced
1 tbsp olive oil
1/2 tbsp lemon juice
Salt and pepper to taste

Directions:
Preheat air fryer to 375°F (190°C).
Sauté spinach, red onion, and garlic in olive oil until softened.
Mix cooked quinoa with sautéed vegetables, feta, lemon juice, salt, and pepper.
Stuff bell peppers with the quinoa mixture.
Air fry stuffed peppers for 12-15 minutes.

Nutritional Info: Approximately 200 calories, 28g carbs, 8g proteins, 9g fats

Lentil and Vegetable Patties

Yield: 2 servings	Prep time: 15 minutes	Cook time: 20 minutes

Ingredients:
1/2 cup cooked lentils
1/4 cup grated carrots
1/4 cup grated zucchini
1 clove garlic, minced
2 tbsp diced onion
2 tbsp whole wheat breadcrumbs
1 egg, beaten
1/2 tsp cumin
1/2 tsp coriander
1 tbsp olive oil

Directions:
Preheat air fryer to 375°F (190°C).
Mix lentils, carrots, zucchini, garlic, onion, breadcrumbs, egg, cumin, coriander, salt, and pepper.
Form mixture into patties and brush with olive oil.
Air fry for 10 minutes on each side.
Serve with cucumber yogurt dip.

Nutritional Info: Approximately 180 calories, 28g carbs, 8g proteins, 5g fats

Air-Fried Portobello Mushrooms

Yield: 2 servings	Prep time: 10 minutes	Cook time: 12 minutes

Ingredients:
2 large Portobello mushrooms
1/2 cup cooked quinoa
2 tbsp chopped parsley
1 clove garlic, minced
2 tbsp diced onion
1 tbsp olive oil
1/4 cup vegetable broth
1/4 tsp thyme
Salt and pepper to taste

Directions:
Preheat air fryer to 375°F (190°C).
Sauté garlic and onion in olive oil until softened.
Mix with cooked quinoa, parsley, thyme, salt, and pepper.
Stuff mushrooms with quinoa mixture.
Air fry for 10-12 minutes.

Nutritional Info: Approximately 230 calories, 32g carbs, 8g proteins, 8g fats

Spaghetti Squash Cakes

Yield: 2 servings	Prep time: 15 minutes	Cook time: 20 minutes

Ingredients:
1/2 medium spaghetti squash
1 egg, beaten
2 tbsp whole wheat flour
2 tbsp grated Parmesan cheese
1 clove garlic, minced
1 tbsp olive oil
1 cup cherry tomatoes, halved
1 tbsp chopped basil
Salt and pepper to taste

Directions:
Cook spaghetti squash and scoop out the flesh.
Mix with egg, flour, and Parmesan cheese.
Form into cakes and air fry at 375°F for 10 minutes on each side.
Sauté garlic and tomatoes with basil for the dipping sauce.
Serve squash cakes with garlic tomato sauce.

Nutritional Info: Approximately 180 calories, 24g carbs, 8g proteins, 7g fats

Cauliflower Steaks

Yield: 2 servings	Prep time: 10 minutes	Cook time: 12 minutes

Ingredients:
1 medium cauliflower, sliced into steaks
1/2 cup Brussels sprouts, halved
1 tbsp olive oil
1/4 cup chopped parsley
2 cloves garlic, minced
1 tbsp red wine vinegar
1/2 tsp oregano
1/4 tsp red pepper flakes
Salt and pepper to taste

Directions:
Preheat air fryer to 400°F (200°C).
Toss cauliflower and Brussels sprouts with olive oil and spices.
Air fry for 10-12 minutes.
Blend parsley, garlic, vinegar, oregano, and red pepper flakes for chimichurri.
Serve with chimichurri sauce.

Nutritional Info: Approximately 170 calories, 14g carbs, 5g proteins, 11g fats

Vegetable and Black Bean Empanadas

Yield: 2 servings | **Prep time:** 15 minutes | **Cook time:** 10 minutes

Ingredients:
4 whole wheat empanada dough discs
1/2 cup black beans, drained and rinsed
1/4 cup diced bell peppers
1/4 cup corn kernels
2 tbsp diced onions
1/2 tsp cumin
1/2 tsp chili powder
1/2 avocado, diced
1 tbsp lime juice
1 tbsp chopped cilantro

Directions:
Preheat air fryer to 375°F (190°C).
Sauté bell peppers, corn, and onions with cumin and chili powder.
Mix with black beans.
Fill empanada dough with mixture and seal edges.
Air fry for 8-10 minutes.
Mix diced avocado, lime juice, and cilantro for salsa.

Nutritional Info: Approximately 240 calories, 34g carbs, 6g proteins, 10g fats

Acorn Squash Rings

Yield: 2 servings | **Prep time:** 10 minutes | **Cook time:** 15 minutes

Ingredients:
1 small acorn squash, sliced into rings
1/2 cup cooked wild rice
2 tbsp dried cranberries
2 tbsp chopped walnuts
1 tbsp olive oil
Salt and pepper to taste
2 cups mixed greens
1 tbsp balsamic vinaigrette

Directions:
Preheat air fryer to 375°F (190°C).
Cook wild rice and mix with cranberries and walnuts.
Brush squash rings with olive oil and air fry for 12-15 minutes.
Fill squash rings with wild rice mixture.
Serve with mixed greens and balsamic vinaigrette.

Nutritional Info: Approximately 250 calories, 36g carbs, 5g proteins, 11g fats

Quinoa and Vegetable Stir-Fry

Yield: 2 servings | **Prep time:** 10 minutes | **Cook time:** 15 minutes

Ingredients:
1 cup cooked quinoa
2 cups mixed vegetables (bell peppers, zucchini, broccoli, carrots, snap peas)
1 clove garlic, minced
1/2 tablespoon olive oil
1/2 tablespoon soy sauce
1/2 teaspoon sesame oil
1/2 teaspoon grated ginger
Salt and pepper to taste
1/2 tablespoon sesame seeds
Fresh cilantro, chopped (for garnish)

Directions:
Preheat air fryer to 375°F (190°C).
Toss mixed vegetables and garlic in olive oil, season with salt and pepper.
Air fry for 10 minutes, shaking halfway through.
In a bowl, mix cooked quinoa and air-fried vegetables.
Add soy sauce, sesame oil, and grated ginger. Toss to combine.
Garnish with sesame seeds and fresh cilantro. Serve warm.

Nutritional Info: Approximately 230 calories, 7g protein, 30g carbs, 9g Fat

DINNER RECIPES

Zucchini Sticks with Pesto Dip

Yield: 2 servings | **Prep time:** 10 minutes | **Cook time:** 10 minutes

Ingredients:
1 large zucchini, sliced into sticks
1/4 cup whole wheat breadcrumbs
2 tbsp grated Parmesan cheese
1 egg, beaten
1/4 cup fresh basil
1 clove garlic
1 tbsp pine nuts
2 tbsp olive oil
Salt and pepper to taste

Directions:
Preheat air fryer to 400°F (200°C).
Dip zucchini sticks in beaten egg and coat with breadcrumbs mixed with Parmesan.
Air fry for 8-10 minutes.
Blend basil, garlic, pine nuts, and olive oil to make pesto.
Serve zucchini sticks with pesto dip.

Nutritional Info: Approximately 220 calories, 12g carbs, 6g proteins, 17g fats

Sweet Potato Hash

Yield: 2 servings | **Prep time:** 10 minutes | **Cook time:** 15 minutes

Ingredients:
1 medium sweet potato, diced
1/2 red bell pepper, diced
1/2 onion, diced
1 stem green onion
1 tbsp olive oil
Salt and pepper to taste

Directions:
Preheat the air fryer to 375°F (190°C).
Toss the diced sweet potato, bell pepper, and onion with olive oil, salt, and pepper.
Place the mixture in the air fryer basket and cook for 15 minutes, shaking halfway through.
Sprinkle diced green onion

Nutritional Info: Approximately 170 calories, 25g carbs, 7g fats

Sweet Potato and Black Bean Tacos

Yield: 2 servings | **Prep time:** 10 minutes | **Cook time:** 15 minutes

Ingredients:
1 medium sweet potato, diced
1/2 can black beans, drained and rinsed
4 whole wheat tortillas
1/2 avocado, sliced
1/2 lime, cut into wedges
2 tbsp chopped cilantro
2 tbsp diced red onion
1/2 tsp cumin
1/2 tsp chili powder
1 tbsp olive oil

Directions:
Preheat air fryer to 400°F (200°C).
Toss diced sweet potato with olive oil, cumin, chili powder, salt, and pepper.
Air fry for 15 minutes, shaking halfway through.
Assemble tacos with black beans, sweet potato, onion, avocado, and cilantro.
Serve with lime wedges.

Nutritional Info: Approximately 220 calories, 10g carbs, 10g proteins, 16g fats

Chickpea and Kale Falafel

Yield: 2 servings | **Prep time:** 10 minutes | **Cook time:** 15 minutes

Ingredients:
1/2 can chickpeas, drained and rinsed
1/2 cup fresh kale, chopped
1 clove garlic, minced
2 tbsp diced onion
1/2 tsp cumin
1/2 tsp coriander
1 tbsp flour
1 tbsp olive oil
2 tbsp tahini
1 tbsp lemon juice

Directions:
Preheat air fryer to 375°F (190°C).
Blend chickpeas, kale, garlic, onion, cumin, coriander, and flour in a food processor.
Form mixture into balls and coat lightly with olive oil.
Air fry for 10-12 minutes.
Mix tahini, lemon juice, and water for the sauce.
Serve falafel with lemon-tahini sauce.

Nutritional Info: Approximately 210 calories, 24g carbs, 7g proteins, 10g fats

Eggplant Parmesan

Yield: 2 servings | **Prep time:** 10 minutes | **Cook time:** 15 minutes

Ingredients:
1 large eggplant, sliced into 1/2-inch rounds
1/2 cup whole wheat breadcrumbs
1/4 cup grated Parmesan cheese
1 teaspoon dried basil
1 teaspoon dried oregano
1/2 cup marinara sauce (low sugar)
1/2 cup mozzarella cheese, shredded
Olive oil spray

Directions:
Preheat the air fryer to 375°F (190°C).
In a bowl, mix breadcrumbs, Parmesan cheese, dried basil, and oregano.
Spray both sides of the eggplant slices lightly with olive oil spray.
Dip each slice into the breadcrumb mixture, pressing lightly to coat.
Place the coated eggplant slices in the air fryer basket in a single layer. Cook for 8-10 minutes, until golden and crispy.
Top each slice with a spoonful of marinara sauce and shredded mozzarella cheese.
Return to the air fryer and cook for an additional 3-5 minutes, until the cheese is melted and bubbly.
Serve warm

Nutritional Info: Approximately 280 calories, 32g carbs, 12g proteins, 12g Fats

BEEF AND PORK

Beef Tenderloin with Broccoli and Bell Peppers

Yield: 2 servings | **Prep time:** 10 minutes | **Cook time:** 17 minutes

Ingredients:

2 (6 oz) beef tenderloin steaks
1 bunch broccoli, cut into florets
1 red bell pepper, sliced
1 tablespoon olive oil
1 teaspoon garlic powder
1 teaspoon paprika
Salt and pepper to taste
1 tablespoon lemon juice
Fresh parsley for garnish

Directions:

Preheat the air fryer to 400°F (200°C).

Rub the beef steaks with olive oil, garlic powder, paprika, salt, and pepper.

In a separate bowl, toss the broccoli florets and bell pepper slices with a little olive oil, salt, and pepper.

Place the steaks in the air fryer basket and cook for 8-10 minutes, flipping halfway through, until desired doneness is reached.

After the steaks are done, remove them from the air fryer and cover with foil to rest.

Add the seasoned vegetables to the air fryer basket and cook for 5-7 minutes, or until tender.

Drizzle lemon juice over the vegetables before serving and garnish with fresh parsley.

Nutritional Info: Approximately 350 calories, 12g carbs, 35g proteins, 18g fats:

Grilled Flank Steak with Asparagus

Yield: 2 servings	Prep time: 15 minutes	Cook time: 10 minutes

Ingredients:
2 flank steak portions (6 oz each)
1 tbsp olive oil
1 tbsp fresh lemon juice
1 garlic clove
1/2 tsp dried oregano
Salt and pepper
1 cup asparagus, trimmed

Directions:
Preheat air fryer to 400°F (200°C).
In a bowl, mix olive oil, lemon juice, minced garlic, oregano, salt, and pepper. Brush the mixture over the flank steaks. Place flank steaks in the air fryer basket and cook for 8-10 minutes, flipping halfway through.
Toss asparagus with olive oil, salt, and pepper, and air fry for 5-6 minutes.
Let steak rest for a few minutes before serving with asparagus.

Nutritional Info: Approximately 280 calories, 5g carbs, 14g fats, 30g protein

Espresso-Spiced Steak

Yield: 2 servings	Prep time: 5 minutes	Cook time: 10 minutes

Ingredients:
3/4 lb lean strip steak
1/4 tbsp ground espresso or instant coffee
1/4 tbsp onion powder
1/4 tbsp smoked paprika
1/4 tbsp chili powder
1/4 tsp brown sugar
1/4 tbsp olive oil

Directions:
Season evenly the steak with the mix of spices and coffee.
Preheat the Air Fryer 400°F (200°C) for about 5 minutes.
Lightly brush the air fryer basket with olive oil to prevent sticking. Place the steak in the basket.
Air fry the steak for 8-10 minutes, depending on the thickness of the steak and your desired level of doneness. Flip the steak halfway through the cooking time.
Rest the steak for 10 minutes. Slice it and serve with tomatoes and air fried cauliflower.

Nutritional Info: Approximately 290 calories, 3g carbs, 40g proteins, 13g fats

Pork Tenderloin with Cauliflower Mash

| Yield: 2 servings | Prep time: 10 minutes | Cook time: 20 minutes |

Ingredients:
1 pork tenderloin (about 1 lb)
1 tbsp olive oil
1 tsp dried oregano
1 tsp dried thyme
1/2 tsp garlic powder
Salt and pepper to taste
2 cups cauliflower florets

Directions:
Preheat air fryer to 400°F (200°C). Rub pork tenderloin with olive oil. Mix oregano, thyme, garlic powder, salt, and pepper, and rub onto the pork.
Place pork in the air fryer basket and cook for 20 minutes, flipping halfway through.
Steam cauliflower until tender, then mash with a bit of olive oil, salt, and pepper.
Serve pork tenderloin with cauliflower mash.

Nutritional Info: Approximately 280 calories, 10g carbs, 30g proteins, 12g fats

Pork Loin with Brussels Sprouts

| Yield: 2 servings | Prep time: 5 minutes | Cook time: 20 minutes |

Ingredients:
2 pork loin chops (6 oz each)
1/2 lb Brussels sprouts, halved
1 tablespoon olive oil
1 teaspoon garlic powder
1 teaspoon dried thyme
Salt and pepper to taste

Directions:
Preheat the air fryer to 375°F (190°C).
Rub pork loin chops with olive oil, garlic powder, thyme, salt, and pepper.
Toss Brussels sprouts with olive oil, salt, and pepper.
Place pork chops and Brussels sprouts in the air fryer basket.
Cook for 15-20 minutes, flipping halfway through, until pork is cooked and Brussels sprouts are crispy.
Serve immediately.

Nutritional Info: Approximately 320 calories, 10g Carbs, 35g Proteins, 15g fats

Pork Chops with Mustard Cream and Zucchini

Yield: 2 servings | **Prep time:** 10 minutes | **Cook time:** 20 minutes

Ingredients:
2 boneless lean pork chops
Salt and pepper
1/2 tsp garlic powder
1/2 tsp onion powder
1/2 tsp paprika
1 tsp olive oil
1/4 cup heavy cream
1 tbsp Dijon mustard
1/2 tsp whole grain mustard
1/2 tsp lemon juice
Salt and pepper
1 medium zucchini, sliced
1 tsp olive oil
Salt and pepper
1/2 tsp Italian seasoning
1 clove garlic, minced (optional)

Directions:
Preheat air fryer to 375°F (190°C).
Season pork chops with salt, pepper, garlic powder, onion powder, and paprika. Rub with olive oil.
Air fry for 10-12 minutes, flipping halfway, until internal temperature reaches 145°F (63°C).
In a small saucepan, combine cream, mustards, and lemon juice. Cook over medium heat until slightly thickened, about 3-5 minutes. Season with salt and pepper.
Toss zucchini with olive oil, salt, pepper, Italian seasoning, and garlic.
Air fry at 375°F (190°C) for 8-10 minutes, shaking halfway through.
Plate pork chops, drizzle with mustard cream sauce. Serve zucchini on the side.

Nutritional Info: Approximately 400 calories, 6g carbs, 35g proteins, 28g fats

FISH AND SEAFOOD

Baked Salmon and Steamed Asparagus

Yield: 2 servings | **Prep time:** 5 minutes | **Cook time:** 12 minutes

Ingredients:	Directions:
2 salmon fillets 1 tbsp olive oil 1 tbsp fresh lemon juice 1/2 tbsp fresh dill, chopped Salt and pepper to taste 1 cup asparagus, trimmed	Preheat the air fryer to 375°F (190°C). Brush salmon fillets with olive oil and lemon juice. Sprinkle with dill, salt, and pepper. Place salmon fillets in the air fryer basket and cook for 12 minutes. Steam asparagus in a steamer or microwave with a bit of water until tender. Serve salmon with steamed asparagus.

Nutritional Info: Approximately 250 calories, 4g carbs, 25g proteins, 14g fats

Seared Tuna Steaks with Stir-Fried Bok Choy

Yield: 2 servings | **Prep time:** 5 minutes | **Cook time:** 8 minutes

Ingredients:	Directions:
2 tuna steaks 1 tbsp olive oil 1/2 tbsp soy sauce (low sodium) 1/2 tbsp sesame seeds 1/2 tsp grated ginger Salt and pepper to taste 2 cups bok choy, chopped	Preheat air fryer to 400°F (200°C). Brush tuna steaks with olive oil, soy sauce, sesame seeds, ginger, salt, and pepper. Place tuna steaks in the air fryer basket and cook for 8 minutes, flipping halfway through. Stir-fry bok choy in a pan with a little olive oil while tuna is cooking. Serve tuna steaks with stir-fried bok choy.

Nutritional Info: Approximately 340 calories, 7g carbs, 40g protein, 14g fats

Shrimp Skewers with Mixed Greens Salad

Yield: 2 servings | **Prep time:** 10 minutes | **Cook time:** 15 minutes

Ingredients:
1/2 lb large shrimp, peeled and deveined
1 tbsp olive oil
1/2 tbsp lemon juice
1 garlic clove, minced
1/2 tsp paprika
Salt and pepper to taste
Skewers
2 cups mixed greens
1/2 cup cherry tomatoes, halved
1/2 cucumber, sliced
1 tbsp olive oil for dressing

Directions:
Preheat the air fryer to 400°F (200°C).
In a bowl, combine olive oil, lemon juice, garlic, paprika, salt, and pepper.
Thread shrimp onto skewers and brush with the olive oil mixture. Place shrimp skewers in the air fryer basket and cook for 8 minutes, turning halfway through.
Toss mixed greens, cherry tomatoes, and cucumber with olive oil dressing while shrimp is cooking.
Serve shrimp skewers with the mixed greens salad.

Nutritional Info: Approximately 200 calories, 5g carbs, 24g proteins, 10g fats

Garlic Butter Baked Cod with Brussels Sprouts

Yield: 2 servings | **Prep time:** 10 minutes | **Cook time:** 15 minutes

Ingredients:
2 cod fillets
1 tbsp butter, melted
1 garlic clove, minced
1/2 tbsp fresh parsley, chopped
Salt and pepper to taste
2 cups Brussels sprouts, halved

Directions:
Preheat air fryer to 375°F (190°C).
Brush cod fillets with melted butter, garlic, parsley, salt, and pepper.
Place cod fillets in the air fryer basket and cook for 15 minutes.
Toss Brussels sprouts with a little olive oil, salt, and pepper, and air fry for 12 minutes, shaking halfway through.
Serve cod with roasted Brussels sprouts.

Nutritional Info: Approximately 280 calories, 14g carbs, 10g fats, 30g protein:

Lemon Garlic Shrimp with Asparagus

Yield: 2 servings | Prep time: 5 minutes | Cook time: 10 minutes

Ingredients:
1 lb large shrimp, peeled and deveined
1 bunch asparagus, trimmed and cut into 2-inch pieces
2 tablespoons olive oil
2 cloves garlic, minced
Juice of 1 lemon
Salt and pepper to taste

Directions:
Preheat the air fryer to 400°F (200°C).
Toss shrimp and asparagus with olive oil, garlic, lemon juice, salt, and pepper.
Place shrimp and asparagus in the air fryer basket.
Cook for 8-10 minutes, shaking the basket halfway through, until shrimp are pink and asparagus is tender.
Serve hot.

Nutritional Info: Approximately 250 calories, 8g carbs, 30g proteins, 10g fats

Salmon with Green Beans

Yield: 2 servings | Prep time: 5 minutes | Cook time: 12 minutes

Ingredients:
2 salmon fillets (6 oz each)
1/2 lb green beans, trimmed
1 tablespoon olive oil
1 teaspoon paprika
1 teaspoon dried dill
Salt and pepper to taste
Lemon wedges for serving

Directions:
Preheat the air fryer to 375°F (190°C).
Rub salmon fillets with olive oil, paprika, dill, salt, and pepper.
Toss green beans with olive oil, salt, and pepper.
Place salmon fillets and green beans in the air fryer basket.
Cook for 10-12 minutes, until salmon is cooked through and green beans are tender.
Serve with lemon wedges.

Nutritional Info: Approximately 320 calories, 7g carbs, 35g proteins, 15g fats

Lemon Garlic Swordfish with Grilled Zucchini

Yield: 2 servings	Prep time: 10 minutes	Cook time: 10 minutes

Ingredients:
2 swordfish steaks
1 tbsp olive oil
1 tbsp fresh lemon juice
1 garlic clove, minced
1/2 tsp dried oregano
Salt and pepper to taste
2 zucchini, sliced

Directions:
Preheat air fryer to 400°F (200°C). Brush swordfish steaks with olive oil, lemon juice, garlic, oregano, salt, and pepper.
Place swordfish steaks in the air fryer basket and cook for 10 minutes, flipping halfway through.
Toss zucchini slices with olive oil, salt, and pepper, and air fry for 8 minutes, shaking halfway through.
Serve swordfish with grilled zucchini.

Nutritional Info: Approximately 310 calories, 8g carbs, 11g fats, 35g proteins

Herb-Crusted Halibut with Cherry Tomatoes

Yield: 2 servings	Prep time: 10 minutes	Cook time: 15 minutes

Ingredients:
2 halibut fillets
1 tbsp olive oil
1/2 tsp dried oregano
1/2 tsp dried thyme
1 garlic clove, minced
Salt and pepper to taste
1 cup cherry tomatoes, halved

Directions:
Preheat air fryer to 375°F (190°C). Brush halibut fillets with olive oil, oregano, thyme, garlic, salt, and pepper.
Place halibut fillets in the air fryer basket and cook for 12-15 minutes.
Toss cherry tomatoes with olive oil, salt, and pepper, and air fry for 5-6 minutes.
Serve halibut with roasted cherry tomatoes.

Nutritional Info: Approximately 220 calories, 6g carbs, 10g fats, 30g protein

POULTRY

Roasted Turkey Breast with Sautéed Spinach

Yield: 2 servings | **Prep time:** 10 minutes | **Cook time:** 25 minutes

Ingredients:
1 turkey breast (about 1 lb)
1 tbsp olive oil
1 tsp dried thyme
1 tsp dried rosemary
1/2 tsp garlic powder
Salt and pepper to taste
2 cups spinach

Directions:
Preheat air fryer to 375°F (190°C). Rub turkey breast with olive oil. Mix thyme, rosemary, garlic powder, salt, and pepper, and rub onto the turkey.
Place turkey in the air fryer basket and cook for 25 minutes, flipping halfway through.
Sauté spinach in a pan with a little olive oil while turkey is cooking.
Serve turkey breast with sautéed spinach.

Nutritional Info: Approximately 250 calories, 3g carbs, 10g fats, 35g protein

Chicken Breast with Steamed Broccoli

Yield: 2 servings | **Prep time:** 10 minutes | **Cook time:** 15 minutes

Ingredients:
2 boneless, skinless chicken breasts
1 tbsp olive oil
1 tbsp fresh lemon juice
1/2 tsp dried thyme
1/2 tsp dried rosemary
1 garlic clove, minced
Salt and pepper to taste
2 cups broccoli florets

Directions:
Preheat air fryer to 375°F (190°C). In a bowl, mix olive oil, lemon juice, thyme, rosemary, garlic, salt, and pepper.
Brush the mixture over the chicken breasts.
Place chicken breasts in the air fryer basket and cook for 15 minutes, flipping halfway through.
Steam broccoli while the chicken is cooking.
Let the chicken rest before serving with steamed broccoli.

Nutritional Info: Approximately 200 calories, 7g carbs, 18g proteins, 9g fats

Lemon Herb Chicken Thighs with Carrots

Yield: 2 servings | **Prep time:** 5 minutes | **Cook time:** 20 minutes

Ingredients:

4 chicken thighs, bone-in, skin-on
2 large carrots, cut into sticks
1 tablespoon olive oil
1 teaspoon dried thyme
1 teaspoon dried rosemary
Juice of 1 lemon
Salt and pepper to taste

Directions:

Preheat the air fryer to 375°F (190°C).
Rub chicken thighs with olive oil, thyme, rosemary, lemon juice, salt, and pepper.
Toss carrot sticks with a little olive oil, salt, and pepper.
Place chicken thighs and carrots in the air fryer basket.
Cook for 18-20 minutes, flipping halfway through, until chicken is crispy and cooked through.
Serve hot.

Nutritional Info: Approximately 380 calories, 10g carbs, 28g proteins, 25g fats

Chicken Drumsticks with Green Beans

Yield: 2 servings | **Prep time:** 5 minutes | **Cook time:** 25 minutes

Ingredients:

4 chicken drumsticks
1/2 lb green beans, trimmed
1 tablespoon olive oil
1/4 cup grated Parmesan cheese
1 teaspoon garlic powder
Salt and pepper to taste

Directions:

Preheat the air fryer to 375°F (190°C).
Rub chicken drumsticks with olive oil, garlic powder, Parmesan cheese, salt, and pepper.
Toss green beans with a little olive oil, salt, and pepper.
Place chicken drumsticks and green beans in the air fryer basket.
Cook for 20-25 minutes, flipping halfway through, until chicken is golden and cooked through.
Serve drumsticks skinless.

Nutritional Info: Approximately 360 calories, 8g carbs, 35g proteins, 20g fats

SNACK RECIPES

Greek Yogurt with Berries

Ingredients:	Directions:
1 cup Greek yogurt, 1/2 cup mixed berries	Mix yogurt with berries. Serve immediately.
Yield: 2 servings | **Prep time:** 2 minutes	**Nutritional Info:** Approximately 150 calories, 15g carbs, 10g protein, 5g fats

Almonds and a Small Apple

Ingredients:	Directions:
2 small apple 30 almonds	Serve 1 apple and 15 almonds per serving.
Yield: 2 servings | **Prep time:** 0 minutes	**Nutritional Info:** Approximately 95 calories, 25g carbs, 1g protein, 0g fat

Cucumber Slices with Hummus

Ingredients:	Directions:
2 cucumber 1/2 cup hummus	Slice cucumbers. Serve with hummus.
Yield: 2 servings | **Prep time:** 2 minutes	**Nutritional Info:** Approximately 100 calories, 12g carbs, 4g proteins, 5g Fats

Hard-Boiled Egg and a Piece of Fruit

Ingredients:	Directions:
1 hard-boiled egg 1 small piece of fruit (e.g., kiwi, peach) Salt and pepper to taste	Boil eggs Peel, cut and salt to taste. Slice kiwi Serve together.
Yield: 2 servings | **Prep time: 20** minutes	**Nutritional Info:** Approximately 120 calories, 15g carbs, 6g protein, 5g fat

Celery Sticks with Peanut Butter

Ingredients:	Directions:
4 celery sticks 2 tbsp peanut butter	Peel celery, cut into pieces. Add peanut butter. Serve immediately.
Yield: 2 servings | **Prep time: 5** minutes	**Nutritional Info:** Approximately 180 calories, 10g carbs, 7g proteins, 14g fats

Carrot Sticks with Greek Yogurt Dip

Ingredients:	Directions:
1 cup carrot sticks 1/4 cup Greek yogurt dip	Serve carrot sticks together with the Greek yogurt dip mixed with herbs and spices
Yield: 2 servings | **Prep time: 2** minutes	**Nutritional Info:** Approximately 100 calories, 12g carbs, 5g protein, 3g fat

Cottage Cheese with Pineapple

Ingredients:	Directions:
1 cup low-fat cottage cheese 1 cup pineapple chunks	Mix cottage cheese with pineapple chunks Serve immediately.
Yield: 2 servings | **Prep time:** 2 minutes	**Nutritional Info:** Approximately 150 calories, 18g carbs, 14g protein, 3g fat

Avocado on Whole Grain Crackers

Ingredients:	Directions:
1/2 avocado 4 whole grain crackers	Mash 1/2 avocado in a small bowl until smooth. Spread on top of the 4 whole grain crackers. Serve immediately.
Yield: 2 servings | **Prep time: 5** minutes	**Nutritional Info:** Approximately 180 calories, 18g carbs, 4g proteins, 12g fats

Kiwi and Greek Yogurt Snack

Ingredients:	Directions:
2 kiwis, peeled and sliced 1 cup Greek yogurt (plain or lightly sweetened) 1 tablespoon honey (optional) A sprinkle of granola (optional)	Peel and slice the kiwis into rounds or wedges. Divide the Greek yogurt into two bowls. Top each bowl with the kiwi slices. Drizzle with honey and sprinkle with granola if desired. Serve immediately
Yield: 2 servings | **Prep time: 5** minutes	**Nutritional Info:** Approximately 150 calories, 22g carbs, 10g proteins, 3g fats

Turkey Roll-Ups

Yield: 2 servings	Prep time: 5 minutes	Cook time: 7 minutes

Ingredients:
3 slices turkey breast
1 slice low-fat cheese
1 tsp mustard
¼ tsp dry greens

Directions:
Place 3 slices of turkey breast on a flat surface. Cut the slice of cheese into 3 strips and place one strip on each turkey slice.
Apply mustard (about 1/3 tsp) on each turkey and cheese slice.
Roll each turkey slice tightly around the cheese and mustard
Preheat Air Fryer: Preheat your air fryer to 375°F (190°C) for 3 minutes.
Place the roll-ups in the air fryer basket in a single layer and cook for 5-7 minutes until the turkey is lightly browned and the cheese is melted.

Nutritional Info: Approximately 120 calories, 2g carbs, 15g proteins, 6g fats

Cucumber and Cottage Cheese Bites

Yield: 2 servings	Prep time: 10 minutes	Cook time: 10 minutes

Ingredients:
1 cucumber, sliced into thick rounds
1/2 cup low-fat cottage cheese
Salt and pepper to taste
1 tbsp olive oil
Cooking spray

Directions:
Preheat the air fryer to 350°F (175°C).
Brush the cucumber slices with olive oil and season with salt and pepper.
Place the cucumber slices in the air fryer basket and cook for 8-10 minutes, or until slightly crispy.
Top each cucumber slice with a spoonful of cottage cheese before serving.

Nutritional Info: Approximately 110 calories, 6g carbs, 8g proteins, 7g Fats

SALAD   RECIPES

Crunchy Cucumber and Avocado Delight

Yield: 2 servings | **Prep time:** 10 minutes

Ingredients:
2 cucumbers, sliced
1 avocado, diced
1/4 cup red bell pepper, diced
2 tbsp lime juice
1 tbsp fresh cilantro, chopped
Salt and pepper to taste

Directions:
In a bowl, combine the cucumbers, avocado, and red bell pepper.
Drizzle with lime juice and sprinkle with cilantro, salt, and pepper.
Toss gently to combine and serve immediately.

Nutritional Info: Approximately 150 calories, 12g carbs, 2g proteins, 1g fats

Edamame with Sesame

Yield: 2 servings | **Prep time:** 10 minutes | **Cook time:** 15 minutes

Ingredients:
1 cup of edamame (fresh or frozen)
1/2 tablespoon sesame oil
1/2 tablespoon soy sauce
1/2 tablespoon rice vinegar
1/2 tablespoon sesame seeds (toasted)
1/2 teaspoon crushed red pepper flakes (optional)
1/2 clove garlic, minced (optional)
Salt to taste

Directions:
Boil 1 cup of edamame for 3-5 minutes, then drain.
Make Sauce: Mix 1/2 tbsp sesame oil, 1/2 tbsp soy sauce, and 1/2 tbsp rice vinegar in a bowl.
Combine: Toss the cooked edamame with the sauce.
Toast 1/2 tbsp sesame seeds in a dry skillet until golden.
Sprinkle toasted seeds over edamame, add salt to taste, and serve.

Nutritional Info: Approximately 143 calories, 10g carbs, 9g proteins, 10g fats

Zesty Citrus Kale and Quinoa Salad

Yield: 2 servings | **Prep time:** 10 minutes

Ingredients:
1 cup cooked quinoa
2 cups fresh kale, chopped
1 orange, segmented
1/4 cup red onion, thinly sliced
1/4 cup cherry tomatoes, halved
2 tbsp fresh lemon juice
1 tbsp olive oil
Salt and pepper to taste

Directions:
In a large bowl, combine the cooked quinoa, kale, orange segments, red onion, and cherry tomatoes.
In a small bowl, whisk together the lemon juice, olive oil, salt, and pepper.
Pour the dressing over the salad and toss to combine.
Serve immediately.

Nutritional Info: Approximately 220 calories, 32g carbs, 7g proteins, 7g fats:

Herbed Chicken and Spinach Toss

Yield: 2 servings | **Prep time:** 10 minutes

Ingredients:
1 cup cooked chicken breast, shredded
2 cups fresh spinach, chopped
1/4 cup grape tomatoes, halved
1/4 cup cucumber, diced
2 tbsp balsamic vinegar
1 tbsp olive oil
1 tsp dried basil
Salt and pepper to taste

Directions:
In a large bowl, combine the chicken, spinach, grape tomatoes, and cucumber.
In a small bowl, whisk together the balsamic vinegar, olive oil, dried basil, salt, and pepper.
Pour the dressing over the salad and toss to combine.
Serve immediately.

Nutritional Info: Approximately 220 calories, 10g carbs, 10g proteins, 16g fats

Lemon-Garlic Shrimp and Zoodle Salad

Yield: 2 servings | Prep time: 10 minutes | Cook time: 10 minutes

Ingredients:
1/2 lb shrimp, peeled and deveined
2 medium zucchinis, spiralized
1 tbsp olive oil
2 tbsp lemon juice
2 garlic cloves, minced
Salt and pepper to taste
Fresh parsley, chopped

Directions:
Preheat your air fryer to 375°F (190°C) for 3 minutes.
In a bowl, mix the shrimp with olive oil, minced garlic, salt, and pepper.
Place the shrimp in the air fryer basket in a single layer and cook for 5-7 minutes, shaking the basket halfway through, until the shrimp are pink and cooked through.
While the shrimp are cooking, spiralize the zucchinis and place them in a large bowl.
Add the cooked shrimp, lemon juice, salt, pepper, and chopped parsley to the zoodles.
Toss everything together until well combined. Serve immediately.

Nutritional Info: Approximately 200 calories, 7g carbs, 24g proteins, 9g fats

Tangy Tomato and Mozzarella Medley

Yield: 2 servings | Prep time: 10 minutes

Ingredients:
2 cups cherry tomatoes, halved
1/2 cup fresh mozzarella balls, halved
1/4 cup fresh basil, chopped
2 tbsp balsamic vinegar
1 tbsp olive oil
Salt and pepper to taste

Directions:
In a large bowl, combine the cherry tomatoes, mozzarella balls, and basil.
In a small bowl, whisk together the balsamic vinegar, olive oil, salt, and pepper.
Pour the dressing over the salad and toss to combine. Serve immediately.

Nutritional Info: Approximately 180 calories, 8g carbs, 8g proteins, 13g fats

Sweet and Sour Apple Walnut Slaw

Yield: 2 servings | **Prep time:** 10 minutes

Ingredients:

1 apple, julienned
1/2 cup shredded cabbage
1/4 cup walnuts, chopped
2 tbsp apple cider vinegar
1 tbsp olive oil
1 tsp honey
Salt and pepper to taste

Directions:

In a large bowl, combine the apple, cabbage, and walnuts.
In a small bowl, whisk together the apple cider vinegar, olive oil, honey, salt, and pepper.
Pour the dressing over the slaw and toss to combine.
Serve immediately.

Nutritional Info: Approximately 210 calories, 20g carbs, 3g proteins, 15g Fats

Vibrant Veggie and Tofu Rainbow Bowl

Yield: 2 servings | **Prep time:** 10 minutes | **Cook time:** 10 minutes

Ingredients:

1 cup firm tofu, cubed
1/2 cup bell peppers, diced (various colors)
1/2 cup red cabbage, shredded
1/4 cup carrot, julienned
1/4 cup cucumber, diced
2 tbsp soy sauce (low sodium)
1 tbsp olive oil
1 tsp sesame seeds

Directions:

Heat the olive oil in a pan over medium heat. Add the tofu and cook until golden brown, about 5-7 minutes.
In a large bowl, combine the cooked tofu, bell peppers, red cabbage, carrot, and cucumber.
Drizzle with soy sauce and sprinkle with sesame seeds.
Toss to combine and serve immediately.

Nutritional Info: Approximately 190 calories, 12g carbs, 10g proteins, 12g fats:

Balsamic Beet and Arugula Refresh

Yield: 2 servings | **Prep time:** 10 minutes

Ingredients:
2 medium beets, roasted and sliced
2 cups arugula
1/4 cup goat cheese, crumbled
2 tbsp balsamic vinegar
1 tbsp olive oil
Salt and pepper to taste

Directions:
In a large bowl, combine the roasted beets, arugula, and goat cheese.
In a small bowl, whisk together the balsamic vinegar, olive oil, salt, and pepper.
Pour the dressing over the salad and toss to combine.
Serve immediately.

Nutritional Info: Approximately 220 calories, 20g carbs, 6g proteins, 13g fats

Fresh Berry and Baby Spinach Fusion

Yield: 2 servings | **Prep time:** 10 minutes

Ingredients:
2 cups baby spinach
1/2 cup strawberries, sliced
1/4 cup blueberries
1/4 cup raspberries
2 tbsp balsamic vinegar
1 tbsp olive oil

Directions:
In a large bowl, combine the baby spinach, strawberries, blueberries, and raspberries.
In a small bowl, whisk together the balsamic vinegar and olive oil.
Pour the dressing over the salad and toss to combine.
Serve immediately.

Nutritional Info: Approximately 140 calories, 20g carbs, 2g proteins, 7g fats

SOUP RECIPES

Zucchini Soup

Yield: 2 servings | **Prep time:** 15 minutes | **Cook time:** 20 minutes

Ingredients:
2 medium zucchinis, chopped
1 small onion, diced
1 clove garlic, minced
1 tbsp olive oil
2 cups low-sodium vegetable broth
1/4 tsp dried thyme
Salt and pepper to taste

Directions:
Preheat air fryer to 375°F (190°C).
Toss zucchinis, onion, and garlic with olive oil. Air fry for 15 minutes until tender.
Blend air-fried vegetables with vegetable broth until smooth.
Season with thyme, salt, and pepper.
Simmer on the stove for 5 minutes before serving.

Nutritional Info: Approximately 90 calories, 12g carbs, 2g proteins, 4g fats

Sweet Potato and Red Pepper Soup

Yield: 2 servings | **Prep time:** 15 minutes | **Cook time:** 25 minutes

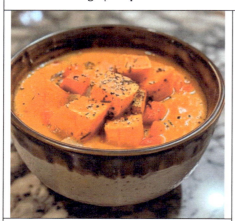

Ingredients:
1 large sweet potato, peeled and cubed
1 red bell pepper, chopped
1 small onion, diced
1 tbsp olive oil
2 cups low-sodium vegetable broth
1/4 tsp smoked paprika
Salt and pepper to taste

Directions:
Preheat air fryer to 375°F (190°C).
Toss sweet potato, red pepper, and onion with olive oil. Air fry for 20 minutes until tender.
Blend air-fried vegetables with vegetable broth until smooth.
Season with smoked paprika, salt, and pepper.
Simmer on the stove for 5 minutes before serving.

Nutritional Info: Approximately 150 calories, 28g carbs, 2g proteins, 5g fats

Spinach and Fennel Soup

Yield: 2 servings	Prep time: 10 minutes	Cook time: 20 minutes

Ingredients:
2 cups spinach leaves
1 small fennel bulb, sliced
1 small onion, diced
1 clove garlic, minced
1 tbsp olive oil
2 cups low-sodium vegetable broth
1/4 tsp fennel seeds
Salt and pepper to taste

Directions:
Preheat air fryer to 375°F (190°C).
Toss fennel, onion, and garlic with olive oil. Air fry for 15 minutes until tender.
Blend air-fried vegetables with vegetable broth and spinach until smooth.
Season with fennel seeds, salt, and pepper.
Simmer on the stove for 5 minutes before serving.

Nutritional Info: Approximately 110 calories, 14g carbs, 3g proteins, 5g Fats

Beet and Carrot Soup

Yield: 2 servings	Prep time: 10 minutes	Cook time: 25 minutes

Ingredients:
2 medium beets, peeled and chopped
2 large carrots, peeled and chopped
1 small onion, diced
1 tbsp olive oil
2 cups low-sodium vegetable broth
1/4 tsp ground cumin
Salt and pepper to taste

Directions:
Preheat air fryer to 375°F (190°C).
Toss beets, carrots, and onion with olive oil. Air fry for 20 minutes until tender.
Blend air-fried vegetables with vegetable broth until smooth.
Season with cumin, salt, and pepper.
Simmer on the stove for 5 minutes before serving.

Nutritional Info: Approximately 130Calories, 24g carbs, 3g proteins, 5g fats

Cabbage and Apple Soup

Yield: 2 servings	Prep time: 15 minutes	Cook time: 25 minutes

Ingredients:
2 cups shredded cabbage
1 apple, peeled and chopped
1 small onion, diced
1 clove garlic, minced
1 tbsp olive oil
2 cups low-sodium vegetable broth
1/4 tsp caraway seeds
Salt and pepper to taste

Directions:
Preheat air fryer to 375°F (190°C).
Toss cabbage, apple, onion, and garlic with olive oil. Air fry for 20 minutes until tender.
Blend air-fried ingredients with vegetable broth until smooth.
Season with caraway seeds, salt, and pepper.
Simmer on the stove for 5 minutes before serving.

Nutritional Info: Approximately 100 calories, 18g carbs, 2g proteins, 4g fats

Butternut Squash and Apple Soup

Yield: 2 servings	Prep time: 15 minutes	Cook time: 15 minutes

Ingredients:
2 cups butternut squash, peeled and cubed
1 apple, peeled and chopped
1 small onion, diced
1 tbsp olive oil
2 cups low-sodium vegetable broth
1/4 tsp ground cinnamon
Salt and pepper to taste

Directions:
Preheat air fryer to 375°F (190°C).
Toss butternut squash, apple, and onion with olive oil. Air fry for 20 minutes until tender.
Blend air-fried ingredients with vegetable broth until smooth.
Season with cinnamon, salt, and pepper.
Simmer on the stove for 5 minutes before serving.

Nutritional Info: Approximately 130 calories, 26g carbs, 2g proteins, 4g fats

Leek and Potato Soup

Yield: 2 servings | **Prep time:** 10 minutes | **Cook time:** 15 minutes

Ingredients:
1 large leek, cleaned and sliced
1 medium potato, peeled and chopped
1 small onion, diced
1 tbsp olive oil
2 cups low-sodium vegetable broth
1/4 tsp dried thyme
Salt and pepper to taste

Directions:
Preheat air fryer to 375°F (190°C).
Toss leek, potato, and onion with olive oil. Air fry for 20 minutes until tender.
Blend air-fried vegetables with vegetable broth until smooth.
Season with thyme, salt, and pepper.
Simmer on the stove for 5 minutes before serving.

Nutritional Info: Approximately 140 calories, 24g carbs, 3g proteins, 5g fats

DESSERT RECIPES

Low-Carb Vanilla Chia Pudding

Yield: 2 servings	Prep time: 10 minutes	Chill time: 4 hours

Ingredients:	Directions:
1 cup unsweetened almond milk 3 tbsp chia seeds 1 tbsp erythritol or your preferred sweetener 1/2 tsp vanilla extract	In a bowl, mix the almond milk, chia seeds, erythritol, and vanilla extract. Stir well and let sit for 5 minutes, then stir again to prevent clumping. Cover and refrigerate for at least 4 hours, or overnight, until the chia seeds have absorbed the liquid and the mixture is thickened. Serve chilled.

Nutritional Info: Approximately 80 calories, 4g carbs, 3g proteins, 6g fats

Chocolate-Dipped Strawberries

Yield: 2 servings	Prep time: 10 minutes	Cook time: 5 minutes

Ingredients:	Directions:
1/2 cup dark chocolate chips (sugar-free) 8 large strawberries	Preheat the air fryer to 350°F (175°C). Melt the chocolate chips in a microwave-safe bowl or using a double boiler. Dip each strawberry into the melted chocolate, allowing the excess to drip off. Place the chocolate-dipped strawberries on a parchment-lined air fryer basket. Cook for 3-5 minutes, just until the chocolate sets. Chill in the refrigerator for 10 minutes before serving.

Nutritional Info: Approximately 100 calories, 10g carbs, 1g proteins, 7g fats

Low-Carb Pumpkin Pie Cups

Yield: 2 servings | Prep time: 10 minutes | Cook time: 15 minutes

Ingredients:
1/2 cup pumpkin puree
1 large egg
2 tbsp erythritol or your preferred sweetener
1/2 tsp pumpkin pie spice
1/4 cup unsweetened almond milk

Directions:
Preheat the air fryer to 320°F (160°C).
In a bowl, mix the pumpkin puree, egg, erythritol, pumpkin pie spice, and almond milk until smooth.
Pour the mixture into small, oven-safe dishes.
Place the dishes in the air fryer and cook for 12-15 minutes, or until set.
Allow to cool slightly before serving.

Nutritional Info: Approximately 70 calories, 8g carbs, 3g proteins, 3g fats

Pear Slices with Almonds

Yield: 2 servings | Prep time: 5 minutes | Cook time: 10 minutes

Ingredients:
1 large pear, sliced
1 tbsp almond butter
1 tbsp slivered almonds

Directions:
Preheat the air fryer to 350°F (175°C).
Arrange the pear slices in a single layer in the air fryer basket.
Drizzle with almond butter and sprinkle with slivered almonds.
Cook for 8-10 minutes, or until the pears are tender.
Serve warm.

Nutritional Info: Approximately 90 calories, 12g carbs, 2g proteins, 5g fats

Low-Carb Lemon Pudding

Yield: 2 servings | **Prep time:** 10 minutes | **Chill time:** 1 hour

Ingredients:	Directions:
1 cup unsweetened almond milk 2 tbsp lemon juice 1 tbsp lemon zest 2 tbsp erythritol or your preferred sweetener 1/2 tsp xanthan gum (thickener)	In a saucepan, heat the almond milk over medium heat until warm. Add the lemon juice, lemon zest, and erythritol, stirring until combined. Sprinkle in the xanthan gum slowly, whisking continuously to avoid clumps. Pour the mixture into ramekins and chill in the refrigerator for at least 1 hour before serving.

Nutritional Info: Approximately 40 calories, 3g carbs, 1g proteins, 2g fats

Coconut Macaroons

Yield: 2 servings | **Prep time:** 10 minutes | **Cook time:** 15 minutes

Ingredients:	Directions:
1 cup unsweetened shredded coconut 2 egg whites 2 tbsp erythritol or your preferred sweetener 1/2 tsp vanilla extract	Preheat the air fryer to 320°F (160°C). In a bowl, beat the egg whites until soft peaks form. Gently fold in the shredded coconut, erythritol, and vanilla extract. Scoop small mounds of the mixture onto a parchment-lined air fryer basket. Cook for 12-15 minutes, or until golden brown. Allow to cool before serving.

Nutritional Info: Approximately 140 calories, 4g carbs, 3g proteins, 12g fats

Cinnamon Nut Clusters

Yield: 2 servings | **Prep time:** 5 minutes | **Cookl time:** 10 minutes

Ingredients:
1/2 cup mixed nuts (almonds, walnuts, pecans)
1 tbsp melted butter
1 tbsp erythritol or your preferred sweetener
1 tsp ground cinnamon

Directions:
Preheat the air fryer to 320°F (160°C).
In a bowl, mix the melted butter, erythritol, and cinnamon.
Add the mixed nuts and toss to coat evenly.
Spread the nuts in a single layer in the air fryer basket.
Cook for 8-10 minutes, shaking the basket halfway through.
Allow to cool before serving.

Nutritional Info: Approximately 180 calories, 5g carbs, 4g proteins, 17g fats

Low-Carb Berry Cheesecake Bites

Yield: 2 servings | **Prep time:** 15 minutes | **Chill time:** 1 hour

Ingredients:
4 oz cream cheese, softened
2 tbsp Greek yogurt
1 tbsp erythritol or your preferred sweetener
1/2 tsp vanilla extract
1/4 cup mixed berries (blueberries, strawberries, raspberries)

Directions:
In a bowl, beat the cream cheese, Greek yogurt, erythritol, and vanilla extract until smooth.
Gently fold in the mixed berries.
Spoon the mixture into silicone molds or small ramekins.
Chill in the refrigerator for at least 1 hour before serving.

Nutritional Info: Approximately 140 calories, 6g carbs, 4g proteins, 12g fats

Low-Carb Chocolate Mug Cake

Yield: 2 servings	Prep time: 5 minutes	Cook time: 10 minutes

Ingredients:
4 tbsp almond flour
2 tbsp cocoa powder (unsweetened)
2 tbsp erythritol or your preferred sweetener
1/4 tsp baking powder
1 large egg
2 tbsp almond milk
1/2 tsp vanilla extract

Directions:
Preheat the air fryer to 350°F (175°C).
In a bowl, mix the almond flour, cocoa powder, erythritol, and baking powder.
Add the egg, almond milk, and vanilla extract to the dry ingredients and mix until well combined.
Divide the batter between two microwave-safe mugs or small ramekins.
Place the mugs in the air fryer and cook for 8-10 minutes, or until a toothpick inserted in the center comes out clean.
Allow to cool slightly before serving.

Nutritional Info: Approximately 180 calories, 6g carbs, 8g proteins, 14g fats

Baked Apples with Cinnamon

Yield: 2 servings	Prep time: 10 minutes	Cook time: 5 minutes

Ingredients:
2 apples
1 tbsp melted butter
1 tbsp sweetener
1 tsp ground cinnamon
¼ cup chopped walnuts

Directions:
Preheat air fryer to 375°F (190°C).
Core the apples and place them in a baking dish.
In a bowl, combine melted butter, sweetener, cinnamon, and chopped walnuts.
Stuff the apples with the walnut mixture.
Air fry for 5 minutes until apples are tender.

Nutritional Info: Approximately 120 calories, 20g carbs, 1g proteins, 5g fats

Apple Cinnamon Chips

Yield: 2 servings | **Prep time:** 5 minutes | **Cook time:** 20 minutes

Ingredients:
2 large apples, thinly sliced
1 tsp ground cinnamon

Directions:
Preheat the air fryer to 300°F (150°C).
Toss the apple slices with cinnamon in a bowl.
Place the slices in a single layer in the air fryer basket.
Cook for 15-20 minutes, shaking the basket every 5 minutes, until the apples are crispy.
Let cool before serving.

Nutritional Info: Approximately 80 calories, 22g carbs, 0g proteins, 0g fats

DRINKS RECIPES

Cucumber Mint Detox Water

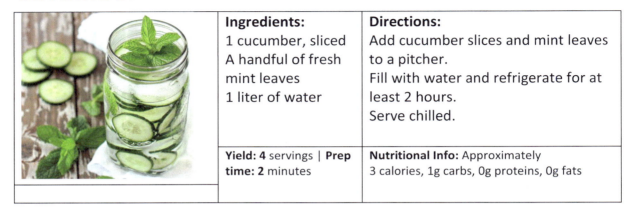

Ingredients:	Directions:
1 cucumber, sliced A handful of fresh mint leaves 1 liter of water	Add cucumber slices and mint leaves to a pitcher. Fill with water and refrigerate for at least 2 hours. Serve chilled.
Yield: 4 servings | **Prep time: 2** minutes	**Nutritional Info:** Approximately 3 calories, 1g carbs, 0g proteins, 0g fats

Cinnamon Spiced Green Tea

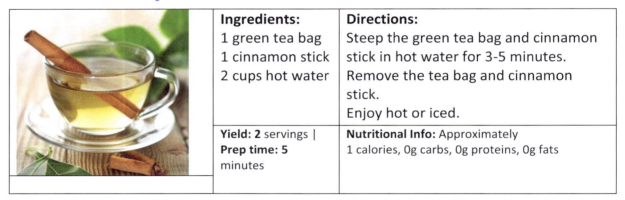

Ingredients:	Directions:
1 green tea bag 1 cinnamon stick 2 cups hot water	Steep the green tea bag and cinnamon stick in hot water for 3-5 minutes. Remove the tea bag and cinnamon stick. Enjoy hot or iced.
Yield: 2 servings | **Prep time: 5** minutes	**Nutritional Info:** Approximately 1 calories, 0g carbs, 0g proteins, 0g fats

Salted Watermelon Agua Fresca

Ingredients:	Directions:
4 cups watermelon, cubed 2 cups water A pinch of sea salt	Blend watermelon and water until smooth. Add a pinch of sea salt and stir. Serve over ice.
Yield: 2 servings | **Prep time: 5** minutes	**Nutritional Info:** Approximately 25 calories, 6g carbs. 1g proteins, 0g fats

Turmeric Golden Milk

Ingredients:	Directions:
2 cups unsweetened almond milk 1 tsp ground turmeric 1/2 tsp ground cinnamon 1/2 tsp ground ginger 2 tsp honey (optional)	Heat almond milk in a saucepan over medium heat. Whisk in turmeric, cinnamon, and ginger until well combined. Add honey if desired. Serve warm.
Yield: 2 servings | **Prep time: 5** minutes	**Nutritional Info:** Approximately 65 calories, 8g carbs, 1g proteins, 3g fats

Lemon Basil Infused Sparkling Water

Ingredients:	Directions:
1 lemon, sliced A handful of fresh basil leaves 1 liter of sparkling water	Add lemon slices and basil leaves to a pitcher. Pour in sparkling water and let it sit for 1-2 hours. Serve cold.
Yield: 2 servings | **Prep time: 2** minutes	**Nutritional Info:** Approximately 3 Calories, 1g carbs, 0g proteins, 0g fats

Berry Bliss Smoothie

Ingredients:	Directions:
1 cup mixed berries (strawberries, blueberries, raspberries) 1 cup unsweetened almond milk 1 banana 2 tbsp chia seeds	Blend all ingredients until smooth. Pour into glasses and enjoy.
Yield: 2 servings | **Prep time: 5** minutes	**Nutritional Info:** Approximately 60 calories, 10g carbs, 1g proteins, 1g fats:

Chia Seed Lemonade

Ingredients:	Directions:
2 lemons, juiced 4 cups water 2 tbsp chia seeds 2 tsp honey (optional)	Mix lemon juice and water in a glass. Stir in chia seeds and let sit for 10-15 minutes. Add honey if desired. Serve cold.
Yield: 2 servings | **Prep time: 2** minutes	**Nutritional Info:** Approximately 30 calories, 5g carbs, 1g proteins, 1g fats

Ginger Zest Herbal Tea

Ingredients:	Directions:
2-inch piece of fresh ginger, sliced 2 herbal tea bags (e.g., chamomile or peppermint) 2 cups hot water	Steep ginger slices and the tea bags in hot water for 5-7 minutes. Remove ginger and tea bags. Enjoy hot or iced.
Yield: 2 servings | **Prep time: 7** minutes	**Nutritional Info:** Approximately 1 calories, 0g carbs, 0g proteins, 0g fats

Almond Vanilla Iced Coffee

Ingredients:	Directions:
2 cups brewed coffee, cooled 1 cup unsweetened almond milk 1 tsp vanilla extract Ice cubes	Mix coffee, almond milk, and vanilla extract in a glass. Add ice cubes. Stir and serve.
Yield: 2 servings | **Prep time: 5** minutes	**Nutritional Info:** Approximately 20 calories, 1g carbs, 1g proteins, 2g fats

Refreshing Aloe Vera Drink

Ingredients:	Directions:
1/2 cup fresh aloe vera gel 2 cups water 2 tbsp lemon juice 2 tsp honey (optional)	Blend aloe vera gel, water, lemon juice, and honey until smooth. Pour into glasses and serve chilled.
Yield: 2 servings | **Prep time: 5** minutes	**Nutritional Info:** Approximately 8 calories, 2g carbs, 0g proteins, 0g fats

Diabetic Food Chart

Diabetic Food Chart

Most Desirable

To Eat

Non-Starchy Vegetables: Broccoli spinach, kale, cucumbers, cauliflower...
Lean Proteins: Chicken breast, turkey, tofu, fish, eggs, legumes...
Whole Grains: Quinoa, brown rice, whole wheat pasta, barley, oats...
Healthy Fats: Avocado, olive oil, nuts...

Fruits: Berries (like strawberries and blueberries), apples, pears, oranges, peaches...
Low-Fat Dairy: Skim milk, low-fat yogurt, cottage cheese...
Beans and Legumes: Lentils, chickpeas, black beans, kidney beans...

Starchy Vegetables: Sweet potatoes, corn, peas, butternut squash...
Whole Grain Breads: Whole wheat bread, whole grain wraps, whole grain tortillas...
Moderate-Fat Dairy: Reduced-fat cheese, low-fat cream cheese...

Red Meat: Beef, pork, lamb (choose lean cuts and limit portions)...
Processed Foods: Canned soups (low sodium), packaged snacks (whole grain or low sugar options)...
High-Sugar Fruits: Grapes, bananas, watermelon (consume in moderation)...

Least Desirable

Refined Grains: White bread, white rice, regular pasta...
Sugary Drinks: Sodas, sweetened fruit juices, energy drinks...
High-Fat and Processed Foods: Pastries, fried foods, chips, full-fat dairy, ice cream...

To Avoid

Creating a Diabetic 7 Day Meal Plan

A Guide to Balanced Eating and Hydration

For optimal blood sugar control, we recommend eating six small meals a day. This approach helps maintain steady energy levels and prevents large fluctuations in blood sugar. Our meal plan includes day-by-day diabetic menus, with slightly larger portions for lunch and dinner, ensuring you feel satisfied throughout the day.

Hydration: The Importance of Pure Water

Staying hydrated is essential for everyone, but it's especially important for those managing diabetes. We recommend drinking pure water every two hours. This practice helps regulate blood sugar levels and supports overall health. Our meal plan tables reflect this recommendation, reminding you to keep hydrated consistently.

In addition to water, low-carb drinks can be enjoyed with your meals if desired. These beverages are a great way to stay hydrated while avoiding unnecessary sugar intake. We suggest options like unsweetened herbal teas or low-carb electrolyte drinks.

Nutritional Balance and Caloric Control

Our meal plan is carefully designed to provide balanced nutrition while keeping daily intake under 1500 calories. The carbohydrate content is evenly distributed throughout the day, helping to maintain stable blood sugar levels. This plan serves as a sample to guide you in creating a personalized meal plan using the recipes data from this cookbook.

Visual Tools and Resources

To assist you in monitoring your nutritional intake, our table includes a visual nutritional chart. This chart highlights if any meals exceed recommended nutritional limits, allowing you to make adjustments as needed. Additionally, there is an automatic corresponding grocery list to reflect ingredients supply for the sample 7-day meal plan.

Customization and Additional Resources

The sample meal plan is just a starting point. We are providing a link to a spreadsheet tool where you can input your own dietary preferences and restrictions into your weekly meal plan from the recipes of this cook book. This tool automatically calculates your grocery list based on your selected meals, making weekly planning a breeze.

Creating a diabetic meal plan doesn't have to be daunting. With the resources provided in this bonus spreadsheet, you can easily customize your meals to meet your needs and preferences. Remember, consistency in meal timing and hydration are key to managing diabetes effectively. Enjoy exploring the variety of delicious and balanced options available in this cookbook!

Our BONUS-
Access to Meal Planner and Grocery List

To access our Google spreadsheet, visit https://tinyurl.com/ymss4m9d or scan the QR code. Remember to make a copy of the spreadsheet for your personal use.

If, for any reasons, you face a problem accessing the spreadsheet, message Bella Flowers on Facebook page **Bella's Cooking**.
Join our Facebook group **Diabetic Air Fryer Recipes**!
If you still have troubles accessing the file, email us:
upparent@gmail.com

7 Day Meal Plan (Sample Table)

Period	Time	Day 1	Day 2	Day 3	Day 4	Day 5	Day 6	Day 7
MORNING	6:30AM	water	water	water	water	water	water	water
	7:00AM	Air Fryer Zucchini Fritters	Air Fryer Veggie Frittata	Fluffy Scrambled Eggs with Spinach and Feta	Almond Flour Waffles	Air Fryer Zucchini Fritters	Fluffy Scrambled Eggs with Spinach and Feta	Air Fryer Veggie Frittata
		Cucumber Mint Detox Water	Lemon Basil Infused Sparkling Water	Chia Seed Lemonade	Cucumber Mint Detox Water	Chia Seed Lemonade	Lemon Basil Infused Sparkling Water	Cinnamon Spiced Green Tea
	10:00AM	Greek Yogurt with Berries	Cucumber Slices with Hummus	Low-Carb Berry Cheesecake Bites	Greek Yogurt with Berries	Cucumber Slices with Hummus	Greek Yogurt with Berries	Cucumber Slices with Hummus
AFTERNOON	12:30PM	water	water	water	water	water	water	water
	1:00PM	Quinoa and Vegetable Stir-Fry	Stuffed Bell Peppers with Quinoa and Spinach	Air-Fried Lentil and Vegetable Patties	Air Fryer Sausage Patties	Quinoa and Vegetable Stir-Fry	Air-Fried Lentil and Vegetable Patties	Stuffed Bell Peppers with Quinoa and Spinach
		Air-Fried Spicy Carrot Ginger Soup	Air-Fried Spicy Carrot Ginger Soup	Air-Fried Cauliflower Soup	Air-Fried Cauliflower Soup	Air-Fried Broccoli Cheddar Soup	Air-Fried Broccoli Cheddar Soup	Air-Fried Tomato Basil Soup
		Cucumber Mint Detox Water	Cinnamon Spiced Green Tea	Chia Seed Lemonade	Chia Seed Lemonade	Refreshing Aloe Vera Drink	Lemon Basil Infused Sparkling Water	Cinnamon Spiced Green Tea
	4:00PM	kiwi	kiwi	Apple	Apple	cracker	kiwi	Apple
EVENING	6:30PM	water	water	water	water	water	water	water
	7:00PM	Chicken Breast with Steamed Broccoli	Baked Salmon with Dill and Steamed Asparagus	Shrimp Skewers with Mixed Greens Salad	Chicken Breast with Steamed Broccoli	Shrimp Skewers with Mixed Greens Salad	Baked Salmon with Dill and Steamed Asparagus	Chicken Breast with Steamed Broccoli
		Zesty Citrus Kale and Quinoa Salad	Zesty Citrus Kale and Quinoa Salad	Tangy Tomato and Mozzarella Medley	Tangy Tomato and Mozzarella Medley	Zesty Citrus Kale and Quinoa Salad	Crunchy Cucumber and Avocado Delight	Zesty Citrus Kale and Quinoa Salad
		Salted Watermelon Agua Fresca	Lemon Basil Infused Sparkling Water	Cinnamon Spiced Green Tea	Cucumber Mint Detox Water	Chia Seed Lemonade	Refreshing Aloe Vera Drink	Turmeric Ginger Golden Milk
	9PM	Air Fryer Low-Carb Chocolate Mug Cake	Air Fryer Baked Apples with Cinnamon	Greek Yogurt with Berries	Low-Carb Berry Cheesecake Bites	Air Fryer Low-Carb Chocolate Mug Cake	Air Fryer Baked Apples with Cinnamon	Low-Carb Lemon Pudding

Daily Calories Chart

Here is the daily macros chart for our sample meal plan. It reflects the total daily nutritional values, and the total amount of calories doesn't exceed 1500. In the bonus Meal Plan Spreadsheet, you'll find this chart automatically updating with your daily meal choices, helping you track calorie intake based on the recipes in this cookbook.

	Day 1	Day 2	Day 3	Day 4	Day 5	Day 6	Day 7
Daily calories	1385 kcal	1321 kcal	1310 kcal	1260 kcal	1368 kcal	1302 kcal	1222 kcal
Daily carbs	156 g	151 g	114 g	89 g	128 g	119 g	140 g
Daily fats	55 g	57 g	66 g	69 g	63 g	62 g	51 g

Detailed Grocery List for a Sample 7 Day Meal Plan

This list created automatically, from the spreadsheet. In brackets we added our notes for shopping convenience.

Bakery
- cracker: 1 Unit (1 box)
- whole wheat breadcrumbs: 4 Tbsp (small package)

Baking Supplies
- almond flour: 6 Tbsp (small package)
- baking powder: 3/4 Tsp (1 can)
- chia seeds: 12 Tbsp (small package)
- cocoa power: 6 Tbsp (small package)
- lemon juice: 20 Tbsp (1 bottle, or 5 lemons)
- lime juice: 2 Tbsp (1 lime)
- sesame seeds: 1 Tbsp (small package)
- thickener (like xanthan gum): 1/2 Tsp (small package)
- vanilla extract: 2 Tsp (small bottle)
- walnuts: 3/4 Cup (1 package)
- whole wheat flour: 1/2 Cup (small package)

Beverages
- sparkling water: 4 liter (2-liter bottles)

Condiments & Oils
- aloe vera gel, fresh: 1 Cup (small bottle)
- balsamic vinegar: 2 Tbsp (small bottle)
- low-sodium soy sauce: 2 Tbsp (small bottle)
- olive oil: 27 Tbsp (bottle)
- sesame oil: 1 Tsp (small package)
- soy sauce: 1 Tbsp (small bottle)

Dairy & Eggs
- almond milk: 2 Cup (1 liter container)
- butter: 3 Tbsp (1 package)
- cheddar cheese: 1 Cup (1 package)
- cream cheese: 4 Oz (small container)
- eggs: 12 Large (1 container)
- feta cheese: 1 1/4 Cup (small package)
- greek yogurt: 6 Cup (3 containers)
- low-fat cheese: 1/2 Cup (small package)
- mozzarella: 1/2 Cup (small package)
- parmesan cheese, grated: 1/2 Cup (small package)
- tofu: 1 Cup (small package)

Dried Beans and Legumes
- Lentils: 1/2 Cup (small package)

Fruits & Vegetables
- apple: 10 pieces (10 apples)
- asparagus: 2 Cup (small bunch)
- avocado: 1 Piece (1 avocado)
- banana: 2 Unit (1 banana)
- basil, fresh: 4 Handful (handful)
- beets: 2 Piece (2 beets)
- bell pepper: 3/4 Cup (2 bell peppers)
- berries, mixed: 3 1/4 Cup (1 package)
- broccoli florets: 4 Cup (1 broccoli)
- carrots: 1/4 Cup (1 lb)
- cauliflower florets: 4 Cup (1 piece)
- cherry tomatoes: 4 Cup (lb)
- cilantro, fresh: 1/2 Cup (1 bunch)
- cucumber: 12 Piece (12 cucumbers)
- dill, fresh: 1 Tbsp (1 bunch)
- garlic: 15 Clove (2 garlics)
- ginger: 2 Inch (I root)
- kale, fresh: 8 Cup (a package)
- lemon zest: 1 Tbsp (1 lemon)
- lemon: 4 Piece (4 lemons)
- mint leaves: 3 Handful
- onion: 7 Small (7 small)
- orange: 4 Piece (1 orange)
- red cabbage: 1/2 Cup (1 cabbage)
- red onion: 1 Cup (1 onion)
- spinach: 4 Cup (1 package)
- tomato: 4 Large (4 Large)
- watermelon: 4 Cup (1 watermelon)
- zucchini: 4 Piece (4 zucchini)

Grains and Rice
- Quinoa: 7 Cup (2 lb)

Health Food
- Hummus: 1 1/2 Cup (1 can)

Meat & Seafood
- chicken breast, boneless, skinless: 4 Piece
- pork, tenderloin: 1 Pound (1 package)
- salmon fillets: 4 Piece (1 package)
- shrimps: 1 Pound (1 package)

Other
- Skewers: 8 Piece

Pantry

    green tea bag: 4 Piece (1 box)
    honey: 18 Tsp (1 large bottle)
    low-sodium vegetable broth:10 Cup (2 boxes)

Spices

    cayenne pepper: 1/2 Tsp (small container)
    cinnamon stick: 4 Piece (
    cinnamon, ground: 3 1/2 Tsp (small   container)
    cumin: 2 1/4 Tsp (small container)
    garlic powder: 1/2 Tsp (small container
    nutmeg: 1/4 Tsp (small container)
    oregano, dried: 1 Tsp   (small container)
    paprika: 1 Tsp (small container)
    rosemary, dried: 1 Tsp(small container)
    salt: 1 Piece   (1 container)
    thyme, dried: 2 Tsp (small container)
    turmeric, ground: 1 tsp (small container)

Appendices

Measurements Conversions

Volume Conversions

1 teaspoon (tsp) = 5 milliliters (ml)

1 tablespoon (tbsp) = 3 teaspoons = 15 ml

1 fluid ounce (fl oz) = 2 tablespoons = 30 ml

1 cup = 8 fluid ounces = 240 ml

1 pint = 2 cups = 480 ml

1 quart = 4 cups = 960 ml

1 liter = 1000 ml = 4.2 cups

Weight Conversions

1 ounce (oz) = 28 grams (g)

1 pound (lb) = 16 ounces = 454 g

1 kilogram (kg) = 1000 g = 2.2 pounds

Temperature Conversions

Celsius to Fahrenheit: $(°C \times 9/5) + 32 = °F$

Fahrenheit to Celsius: $(°F - 32) \times 5/9 = °C$

Common Ingredient Substitutes

Baking Substitutes

Flour: For gluten-free options, use almond flour, coconut flour, or a gluten-free flour blend. Note that ratios may differ (e.g., 1 cup all-purpose flour ≈ 1/4 cup coconut flour).

Sugar: Use equal amounts of natural sweeteners like stevia, erythritol, or monk fruit sweetener.

Honey or maple syrup can also be used, but reduce the liquid in the recipe accordingly.

Butter: Substitute with coconut oil, olive oil, or vegan margarine in equal amounts. For a lower-fat option, use applesauce or mashed banana (1 cup butter = 1/2 cup fruit puree).

Dairy Substitutes

Milk: Replace cow's milk with almond milk, soy milk, oat milk, or coconut milk in a 1:1 ratio.

Cream: Use coconut cream or cashew cream for a dairy-free alternative, or blend silken tofu with a bit of water for a creamy texture.

Cheese: Nutritional yeast can provide a cheesy flavor without the dairy. Vegan cheese options are also widely available.

Eggs

Eggs: For baking, use flaxseeds or chia seeds mixed with water (1 tbsp seeds + 3 tbsp water = 1 egg). Applesauce or mashed banana can also work as egg substitutes, particularly in sweet recipes.

Meat Substitutes

Ground Meat: Replace with lentils, chickpeas, or a plant-based ground meat alternative. Tofu, tempeh, and mushrooms can also provide a similar texture and protein content.

These substitutes are helpful for those with specific dietary needs, and for anyone looking to experiment with different ingredients. They

Recipes and Ingredients Index

Made in United States
Cleveland, OH
01 May 2025

16564322R00042